LORD, I'M LISTENING

From His Heart To Your Heart—
Over 100 Messages From Our King!

One Listener

WESTBOW
PRESS
A DIVISION OF THOMAS NELSON

WestBow Press books may be ordered through booksellers or by contacting:

WestBow Press
A Division of Thomas Nelson
1663 Liberty Drive
Bloomington, IN 47403
www.westbowpress.com
1-(866) 928-1240

ISBN: 978-1-4497-3099-4 (sc)
ISBN: 978-1-4497-3100-7 (hc)
ISBN: 978-1-4497-3098-7 (e)

Library of Congress Control Number: 2011960329

Printed in the United States of America

WestBow Press rev. date: 09/18/2013

This book is dedicated to the honor and glory of our Lord and Savior, JESUS CHRIST. Without HIS presence in us our life would be complete futility.

A very special thanks to my wonderful husband, whose love, support, and encouragement is a gift from God to me. How blessed I am to share my life with you!

Introduction

When I was twenty nine years old a miracle occurred in my life. I had a wonderful job with an airline company, and traveled extensively, but I didn't know why I felt unfulfilled. One day, while reading a book called The Late Great Planet Earth by Hal Lindsey, I came to a sentence that read, "If you have never asked Jesus to come into your life, why don't you put this book down now and do it"? At first I thought this sounded very strange. My next reaction was, "What do I have to lose"? I put the book down and asked Jesus to come into my life and make Himself known to me. I asked Him to forgive me from all the ways my life was contrary to a life holiness. Somehow I knew at that moment my life would never be the same again. And it still remains true today, almost forty years later: My life has never been the same. I experienced the love of Christ in a personal way. I found that the Savior of the world cares deeply for our individual lives.

Shortly thereafter I began reading God's Word, the Bible. I became involved in a Christian church and joined a prayer group. While in prayer, during my personal "quiet time", I would sometimes write letters to the Lord concerning the things that were going on in my life at that particular time. Occasionally I would sense the Lord wanting to speak to my heart concerning those things, so I would write down the words I heard. Contained in this book are the messages I received from the Lord.

As the years came and went I felt these messages were to be shared, as I believe they can apply to anyone's life.

These messages have been a real source of encouragement, inspiration, and strength for me. I pray they will be the same for you!

Here is an invitation for you to receive a Miracle in your life:

> Lord Jesus, I want to know You in a personal way. Please come into my life and make Yourself known to me. I make You the Lord and Savior of my life. I ask You to forgive me from all my sinful ways. I ask that Your Holy Spirit would help me to live a life that honors you! In Jesus Holy Name, I pray, Amen.

Contents

I. Comfort

II. Encouragement

III. Hope

IV. Strength

V. Freedom

VI. Peace

VII. Security

VIII. A Helper

IX. Truth

X. Protection

XI. Confidence

I

Comfort

Be still

and know

I am God.

Be still ... be still.

I am God.

I am in control

of all.

Be still.

2. I AM GETTING YOU READY

And I give them eternal life, and they shall never perish; neither shall anyone snatch them out of My hand John 10:28, NKJV.

You are My own. You belong to Me. I have purchased you with My own life. Why do you persist in not believing My hand is upon all you do? Not one iota is allowed to happen to you without My permission. I see all, hear all, and love all of you unconditionally. Be patient with Me and yourself. I am getting you ready for My return.

3. YOUR HAPPINESS COMES THROUGH ME

Trust in the Lord
with all your heart
and lean not on
your own understanding Proverbs 3:5, NKJV.

*D*o you think for a minute I would not want to talk with you? I am here with you. I am living in you. I was pleased when you spoke of Me today. You were drawn to the ones there I wanted you to speak to. Do not hold grudges against anyone, no matter what you think they say or think about you. I am working always through you, and I cannot use you when you hold grudges or think of your own life's happiness. Remember, your happiness comes from Me, your Father, who loves you more than anyone could ever possibly love you. I will make you happy doing My will for your life. Don't delay. Seek My will for your life. Pray that My Spirit will show you. He will direct you and guide you along the path I want you to take. My Spirit, who moves in My people, is always gentle and loving. He will show you much. Without Him, we cannot work through you, so you must want to yield. I can tell you this: My Spirit is strong, sure, and gentle. He will never push or force His way through you. Pray often for others who need the strength of My Spirit.

4. YOU SHALL LACK NO GOOD THING

Delight yourself also in the Lord,
and He shall give
you the desires of your heart Psalm 37:4, NKJV.

You may not show your disappointment, but My heart sees all and knows the delicate temperament you have. Don't fret or fear the affairs of your life. My children shall not lack any good thing. I will supply for them their most fervent needs and desires. Be gentle with yourself, as I am answering your needs every day you breathe. You are being made whole, strong, courageous, steadfast, and ready—ready for My triumphant return. Remember how special you are to Me. Each of My own is very special to Me, because each one looks to Me for all of his or her needs. This pleases Me and makes My heart glad. When it is hardest to trust Me, I will pray for your strength to trust, as I did for My servant, Peter. Again I say, be truly glad for all I have in store for you.

5. YOU NEEDN'T FEAR

No good thing
will He withhold
from those who walk uprightly   Psalm 84:11, NKJV.

*Y*ou lack nothing for My work. You are chosen, anointed, Spirit-filled, separate, and free—free from worldly ties. All My people are. The world will try to put its hold on you. My Spirit is hovering over you to see to it you will not stray. Trust Me to guide you, love you, and see you through. I am here. You needn't fear the future or anything. My promises are yours, and I will fulfill all your needs. You must trust patiently.

6. DON'T HOLD BACK

Be strong and of good courage, do not fear nor be afraid of them; for the Lord your God, He is the One who goes with you Deuteronomy 31:6, NKJV.

I am as interested in your life as you are. Leave all to Me, and all will be well with you. My promises will reveal to the world My loving concern and care for people's lives. Because I live, you live! All lives are open to Me; don't hold back or be afraid to speak of Me. You must yield to My Spirit's holy leading. All lives are crying for something to hold on to—to know what is real and able to sustain them. My people must draw together before Me and seek Me to know My leading. The world is desperate for the one thing that only I can give it. Be free, be holy, and be Mine. I am leading you.

7. COME TO ME

Come to Me, all you who labor
and are heavy laden,
and I will give you rest   Matthew 11:28, NKJV.

*C*ome to Me for all your needs; come to Me with your heartaches, confusion, denial, and hopelessness. I have a plan for all My own—for all who call Me Lord! My children will need the closeness of one another—not only for support, but also for encouragement and help. I will call many of you for this work. Be prepared and ready to be willing to suffer lack of convenience and comfort for My sake and the sake of one another.

8. BE OPEN

*Be anxious for nothing, but in everything by prayer
and supplication, with thanksgiving, let your requests
be made known to God; and the peace of God, which
surpasses all understanding, will guard your hearts
and minds through Christ Jesus Philippians 4:6–7, NKJV.*

Where do you think I am? I am here with you. Trust in Me to lead you for your life. It means more to Me than you can ever imagine. I will send you to many places and to many people who are afraid to know about Me. I want you to trust Me and not be afraid. I have the power of the universe under My domain. You will be surprised by all that I will show you. I need you to be open in mind and heart to do all that I have for you to do in My plan. I know you are wondering many things, but you must be patient and not get ahead of My plan for your life. You must watch and be watchful of the evil one. He wants to destroy My plan. But I will succeed, for I have overcome the world! You must be watchful of others who want to deceive you. I will guard you and guide you always. I love you with a tender love. Don't be anxious. Be patient. Be kind to others. I will show you much of My ways in others so you will become more like Me. Come to Me often, for I love you.

9. DOUBTS AND FEARS

There is no fear in love;
but perfect love casts out fear,
because fear involves torment   1 John 4:18, NKJV.

*D*o not fear when I want very much to speak with you. Are you not My own, whom I love, died, and live for? You must not fear when you know how much I love you and am concerned for your life. Your life is actually My life now. Your doubts and fears do not come from Me. How I long to fulfill the desires of your heart. How I long to mold you into the person I've created you to be from all eternity. You will see mighty and joyous happenings still to come with your loved ones. They are being wooed by My Spirit. Your prayers and faith in Me exalt Me and My Father. It is because of this that your prayers are visible before your very eyes. Greater works than these shall you see and do, because you glorify the Father and Me.

10. MEET ME

Fear not, for I am with you; be not dismayed,
for I am your God. I will strengthen you, yes,
I will help you, I will uphold you with My
righteous right hand   Isaiah 41:10, NKJV.

I am here with you. You are in My hands. I am controlling your affairs. I am working through you. Continue to meet Me in your quiet time. It will give you an atmosphere of peace in order to stay calm. The world will try to buffet you, but I am your controller. Don't get down about your so-called failures. There are no failures when I am controlling you. Just go one step at a time. Keep close to Me.

11.   ALL YOU WILL FIND

Their Redeemer is strong;
the Lord of hosts is His name   *Jeremiah 50:34, NKJV.*

I am
your Redeemer.
Come to Me when you
are lonely,
confused,
misdirected,
feeling abandoned,
forsaken,
and forgotten.
You will find
all you need in Me.
I am all
in all
for you.
Rely on Me.

II

Encouragement

12. I AM WITH YOU

*Be still
and know
that I am God*   Psalm 46:10, NKJV.

*Do you not see
how I long
    to talk with you
and be near you?
    Any time is right
as long as you
    are willing.
Be still from
    all your cares
        and worries.
I am with you.*

13. FEAR OF OTHERS

For whoever desires to save his life will lose it, but whoever loses his life for My sake will find it Matthew 16:25, NKJV.

S tand by Me, and nothing or no one will harm you. Do not fear others. They cannot touch those whose lives are in My power. Allow Me to let My power flow easily through you. Don't fret for your life. I've told you to trust Me, look to Me, and have Me lead the way. You may not be in any one place for long, but I'm leading you. Do your best to get along—to let others see Me through your life. It needn't be a direct witness. They will see and know who lives in you. Don't hesitate to let others see your beliefs. I love you.

14. LOOK TO ME

*And you shall know the truth, and the truth
shall make you free John 8:32, NKJV.*

Yes, you want to hear from Me as much as I want to speak to you. I want to be near you even more than you know! It is I who speaks. Don't doubt Me; it is I. You mustn't get confused, doubtful, and upset at things you hear others say. You must know what I told you. The evil one is going to try to harass you to get you discouraged and confused. Look to Me. Always look to Me—especially at times of doubt or concern. I will always comfort you and straighten your paths. Read My Word often; it will be your source of strength and guidance. My Word was written for that reason. Now comfort yourself in My words. Know it is I who speaks to you. Pray often, and pray hard for others.

15. STEP BY STEP

But the Lord is faithful, who will establish you and guard you from the evil one 2 Thessalonians 3:3, NKJV.

My Spirit controls the universe. He certainly can control and direct you if you allow Him. I love you, and you will begin to know and understand more deeply now My love for you. You must ask Me for help, and I will be there every step with you. The way seems unclear, but I will move with you step by step, unraveling the way as we go.

16. TRUST ME TO SUPPLY

And we know that all things work together for good to those who love God, to those who are the called according to His purpose Romans 8:28, NKJV.

*D*o you think I cannot come to you at any time and be near you? I am here with you. This day is yours; I've given it to you—another day to mold you, shape you, and draw you closer to Me. I am pleased with you, as always, and want you to be ever so close to Me. I can help you with your insecurities, which are really the insecurities many of My children have.

When you are filled to overflowing, like now, that overflowing joy will spill over onto other lives. I love you. You know I do, but you will know even more as we go on together. Don't allow anyone to remove the joy and peace I place within My children who know Me. Tell others that joy can be given to them. It is theirs for the asking. I will not leave you—this day or any other day. You want very much to hear more, and I have much more for you. In time—My own time—you will receive more. Just know I am near you always, and I love you. I will never run out of things to say to My own.

You must trust in Me for everything: your life, your breath, your health. Know that I give these to you for the purpose of using you to the fullest. I will supply you with all things, but remember to trust Me to supply your needs. I know them well, and I give to you abundantly, so know your heavenly Father will clothe you, shelter you, protect you, and love you always, no matter what happens. When you draw close to Me, I will draw close to you; this is for sure. All things work together for good for those who love Me and try to follow My plan for their lives. Stay close. Follow Me above and before anything and anyone, and you will not stumble. I am your light that shines for you in darkness. Follow Me.

17. YOU MATTER

Let us hold fast
the confession of our hope
without wavering,
for He who promised is faithful   Hebrews 10:23, NKJV.

You needn't go by your feelings. They can change with the wind. Be still and receive Me. I will cause you to be still. I understand your negative thoughts about yourself and others. Remember, the garbage must come up so that it can then get out. It's not pleasant, but remember, it's the only way. Do not condemn yourself. Let Me take care of the affairs of other's lives. This is not your job. You are Mine to be used for My purpose. Joys fulfilled are waiting for you. You needn't fear; I am in control of your affairs. I see all, know all, and allow all to happen to you … and yes, I love you. Be still. Give your cares and concerns to Me to handle; it is My job. Your life is My concern as if no one else mattered. Each life given to Me is important to Me—as if no one else mattered. I speak to you because I love you. You matter to Me—your Lord, God, Savior, friend—I care for you.

18. DYING OF THIRST

*You will keep him in perfect peace, whose
mind is stayed on You Isaiah 26:3, NKJV.*

*L*isten closely to cries of people who lash out—who think they
are hurting you when it's themselves they are hurting. My love
dwells in you. Give it freely, for there is no end to My supply! You
know the desperation of the ones who seek My love. It is as if they
are dying of thirst. Help them and give them something to drink. I
am your source of inner strength and stability. You have My strong
conviction in your heart of what is right and what things are wrong.
Don't let anyone fool you. You have My peace of mind and heart
that all men search for through life. Don't ever abuse it. It is to be
used for My honor and glory.

19. YOU SHALL KNOW

This also comes from the Lord of hosts, who is wonderful in counsel and excellent in guidance Isaiah 28:29, NKJV.

Be still and know that I am God.

You shall hear;
you shall know without a shadow of doubt
My leading—My guiding.

In all your ways, acknowledge Me,
and I will direct your path.

20. HOPE ON

That by two immutable things, in which it is impossible for God to lie, we might have strong consolation, who have fled for refuge to lay hold of the hope set before us Hebrews 6:18, NKJV.

(The following was received immediately after the World Trade Center disaster in New York City on September 11, 2001.)

My children, hope on. Hope in Me. I am your Father. Nothing can hurt you, because you belong to Me. The world is scrambling; the nation weeps. I am God—your God. Hope on in Me. Stay close to Me. I am your lifeline. I am your Father. Pray for those who don't know Me. Pray for them. Pray for all peoples. I love you.

21. ALL IS PLANNED

Let not your heart be troubled; you believe in God, believe also in Me John 14:1, NKJV.

My peace I give to you. Let not your heart be troubled, neither let it be afraid. In My Father's house are many mansions. I have prepared one for you, that where I am, you may be too. Trust me to see you through; keep steadily moving along the path I have set for you. Keep close to Me. I will move you steadily along the path I have for you. You are being kept by Me. You are being made strong by Me. Don't be anxious for anything. All is planned by Me. I and My Father are one. My Spirit is directing your affairs. My people are being made ready and strong by My Spirit.

III

Hope

22. ASK FOR MORE LOVE

In this is love, not that we loved God, but that He loved us, and sent His Son to be the propitiation for our sin 1 John 4:10, NKJV.

Peace—be still. Know that I am God. Besides Me, there is no other. My Spirit leads gently. My Spirit leads assuredly. My Spirit leads safely, knowingly. My Spirit leads peacefully. Perfect love casts out all fear. Fear involves torment. Ask for more love. Love Me more. Experience rapturous love in My presence. I will lead you gently, assuredly, safely, and knowingly. Come to Me. I will calm all your fears.

23. DON'T COMPARE

For we dare not class ourselves or compare ourselves with those who commend themselves. But they, measuring themselves by themselves, and comparing themselves among themselves, are not wise 2 Corinthians 10:12, NKJV.

*Y*ou cry out for more provisions, more income, more benefits, more room, a bigger house—all these I have given you in abundance. You must enjoy what you already have. You have much to be grateful for—abundance, pressed down and running over. You are constantly comparing yourself with others. My Spirit has His set purpose for each life. One life He uses for this set purpose and another for that set purpose. You cannot compare, because this is My will for you now. Appreciate all that I give you—a home; wants, desires, and needs met; and more. I am in control of all that you do. Trust Me, praise Me, thank Me, and look to Me. Love is the richest gift. If you receive a gift in love, nothing else matters.

I love you.

24. I AM THE BURDEN-BEARER

*Draw near to God and He will draw
near to you James 4:8, NKJV.*

*T*he way seems uncertain. You cannot see up ahead, but I am there. I will be with you the whole way. When fears about the future arise, hand them to Me; don't hold on to them. Your fears for today and your worries about tomorrow are not from Me. I want My children happy and trusting, just as a child is with his or her loving parents. I am molding you. You may not see it, but you are being set free every day more and more. You are blessed. Draw near always to Me, and I will be right there with you. I love you.

25. I KNOW WHAT'S BEST FOR YOU

However, when He, the Spirit of truth, has come, he will guide you into all truth … He will glorify Me, for He will take of what is Mine and declare it to you John 16:13–14, NKJV.

*T*he way seems long and laborious, but trust Me to hold you, lead you, and protect you. Why weary yourself with what you feel you cannot do? All it takes is a look from you to Me, and I pick up the burden from you and carry it. Your frame may be weak, but I am making you strong. You may not see it, but you are being tested as gold in the crucible. I am melting away all the dross in your life so that you will be purified in and through Me. Yes, you need to rest a while apart from the noise and restlessness of the world around you, stay with Me, and be refreshed. I will never give you more than you will be able to handle. Hand over to Me all that you can and cannot handle. I sort out each and direct it as best for all involved—especially for you. I love you, and I know what's best for you. My Spirit will lead you, guide you, protect you, and glorify Me through you. Hold on to your Father's hand. He loves you. We love you. Step out in faith and trust.

26. ASK ME TO GUIDE YOU

In quietness
and confidence
shall be
your strength Isaiah 30:15, NKJV.

*T*rust in Me. The way may be short or long, smooth or stony, but My Spirit is with you all the way. I will direct your path as I did with My servants of old. I am no different now than I was then. I still can remove mountains for you. Put yourself and your loved ones in My hands. Trust in Me. I am leading you step by step. Ask Me to guide you. I will show you the direction to take. In quietness and in confidence is your strength. Draw near to Me, and I will draw near to you. Heap upon Me all your confusions, anxieties, doubts, guilt, and fears. Trust Me to see you through. I am with you every step of the way. Put all your concerns in My hands. Trust Me to help you.

27. VALLEY OF DEATH

Yea, though I walk through the valley of the shadow of death, I will fear no evil Psalm 23:4, NKJV.

When you walk through the valley of death, I will be with you. I will uphold you, strengthen you, and help you. Fear no evil, for I am with you. Fear involves torment. Fight fear with My love. My perfect love casts out all fear. You are Mine. I plan the way. You are learning this. Give Me your time—your days. I will plan them. Ask Me. The way is planned for you. I am Lord of your days and your life. Stay near to Me, My children. My love will heal you, help you, draw you to Me, show you the way, keep you, instruct you, deliver you from evil, uphold you, consume you, rapture you, and encompass you, because I am love. My love will always be there for you. Remember this always. I love you.

28. I AM NOT THE AUTHOR OF CONFUSION

But from there you will seek the Lord your God,
and you will find Him if you seek Him with all your
heart and with all your soul Deuteronomy 4:29, NKJV.

Y̶ou will not get confused. I am not the author of confusion. My Spirit will lead and guide, because I control all. I alone am God.

Look to Me for shelter and protection—not only for yourself, but also for all those near and dear to you. Put them under the shadow of the Most High—not only physically, but also in every other way. I am leading you and guiding all you do. Look for Me in all you do. Then you will see Me and find Me in all you do. Those who seek Me shall find Me.

29. THE SATISFIER

'And My people shall be satisfied with My goodness,' says the Lord Jeremiah 31:14, NKJV.

L isten for Me. I will allow you to hear Me. Keep looking; keep listening. My Spirit speaks softly, but clearly. You are being led, guided, protected, and directed by Me. You are Mine. I love you. I need you. My poor, sick, tired, troubled, hungry world needs you. People are hungry, and they don't know what will satisfy them. Nothing will satisfy except the Satisfier. I am the Satisfier. I satisfy completely, assuredly, and to the needs and desires of all. Come to Me, all you who are heavy laden, and I will give you rest. I alone will satisfy every need. Tell them. Tell them.

Jesus

30. ABIDE IN ME

I am the vine, you are the branches. He who abides in Me, and I in him, bears much fruit; for without Me you can do nothing John 15:5, NKJV.

*B*e still and know that I am God. I have gone ahead and prepared the soil for your growth—your fruit. I alone can make the fruit grow. Abiding in Me makes the fruit grow. Resting in Me makes the fruit grow. So rest, abide, and bask in My sunshine. My sunshine is My love. Rest, abide, and grow in Me. Let Me be Lord of all your affairs. I alone can bring order and harmony. I alone can bring growth. This is your desire. This, too, is My desire—to see you happily and joyfully trusting Me for all. I love you.

31. I HAVE OVERCOME THE WORLD

These things I have spoken to you, that in Me you may have peace. In the world you will have tribulation; but be of good cheer, I have overcome the world John 16:33, NKJV.

*M*y peace I give to you—not as the world gives. Yes, in the world, you shall have tribulation and distress, but be of good cheer, for I have overcome the world. You sit here, amazed as to all that has happened. Through prayer and supplication, with thanksgiving, all has worked out in a harmonious and orderly way. I am God Almighty. Before Me there shall be no other gods. Trust Me absolutely.

IV

Strength

32. YOU WILL GROW LESS FEARFUL

Fear not, for I am with you; be not dismayed, for I am your God. I will strengthen you, yes, I will help you. I will uphold you with My righteous right hand Isaiah 41:10, NKJV.

You worry and fret when things are in a state of turmoil in your life. You then turn to Me and ask for help. But each time you turn to Me, you will grow less and less fearful and agitated, because I will remind you of how I worked things out in the past for you. This will honor Me, because your trust will grow stronger and stronger each time. Only perfect trust can keep you calm. I am strengthening you. I am upholding you with My righteous right hand. Nothing is too difficult for Me. I love you.

33. FURTHER BLESSINGS ARE COMING

But seek first the kingdom of God and His righteousness, and all these things shall be added to you Matthew 6:33, NKJV.

See My provisions—even for the birds. My children never lack anything—only their ability to see it. Out of My storehouse are all the riches one could possess if only you realized it. My blessings are abundant and rich. Just have a glad and grateful heart. I will give you this for the asking. You must see how truly blessed you are in order to be further blessed. You lack nothing. You are truly blessed beyond measure with many blessings from Me. I will supply all your needs according to My riches in glory. Have a thankful heart always. Further blessings are coming. My children shall never lack any good thing, if only they have a thankful heart for the blessings I have already given to them. Seek first My kingdom and My righteousness, and all these other things shall be added to you also.

34. BE HAPPY FOR ALL I HAVE FOR YOU

'For I know the plans I have for you,' declares the Lord, 'plans to prosper you and not to harm you, plans to give you hope and a future' Jeremiah 29:11, NIV.

You are My own—My delight. I long to give you your heart's desire. Believe in My providence; believe in My care. You are being led in a definite way. I see up ahead. I know the plans I have for you—plans to prosper and not to harm you, to give you a future and a hope. Go along and be very happy for all I have for you. Trust Me for all. Be joyful for all I have in store for you. Great is My joy. Delight in Me. Ask Me, and I will show you.

35. I NEED YOU

When You said, 'Seek My face,' my heart said to you, 'Your face, Lord, I will seek' Psalm 27:8, NKJV.

Seek Me in all My ways. Look for Me wherever you go. I am there. I am with you. Why do I need you? I need you to help build My kingdom. I need you, just as you need Me. I created you for a higher purpose. You must look to no other—only Me—as your life source. Remember, I will sustain you; I will uphold you. I will be with you wherever you go—wherever you are. I am your light. I am your source. I am your all. I am with you. Trust Me absolutely.

36. I HAVE A WORK FOR YOU

If God is for us, who can be against us?
Romans 8:31, NKJV.

In all your ways, acknowledge Me, and I will direct your path. Behold, I make all things new. You are entering a mountain climb where there are steep steps and fallen rocks. Don't fear. You will be made stronger—more durable physically as well as spiritually. I am becoming more to you than ever before. I am getting you ready for all My works. I have a work for you to do. You can't fail Me, because I will be with you, encouraging you along the way, blessing your work, and sustaining your work. Behold, I make all things new. Go forward unafraid, for I am with you. You will see much. You will see Me at every level. Why do you worry? Why do you doubt Me? Can't you see all I have done in your life up until now? You are called, chosen, and accepted by Me. No man can thwart My plans. I am a holy God. Be holy in all you do, for I am holy. Ask for My help to live out your walk with Me. Keep asking. I am for you; who can be against you? You are Mine. Remember that. I love you.

37. YOU ARE NOT AT THE MERCY OF FATE

In all your ways acknowledge Him, and He shall direct your paths Proverbs 3:6, NKJV.

ust as you need Me, so I need you. My poor world needs you. You are not at the mercy of fate, but you are being led in a clear path with My hand controlling, leading, and guiding. Trust Me absolutely. I will only allow My set purpose for your life. You are being led in a clear and definite way. I am with you. My Spirit is with you. I have much in store for you. Only a little at a time can you handle. Therefore, I will give you a little at a time. Be very happy for all I have in store for you. Trust Me.

38. HEAP UPON ME

My people
are destroyed
for lack
of knowledge   Hosea 4:6, NKJV.

My children are struggling, because they look to themselves for answers. My people perish for lack of knowledge of Me. Heap upon Me all your confusions, anxieties, doubts, guilt, and fears. My people look to themselves for answers. I want you to trust Me to see you through. When I see you set free to be used for Me, I can count the stars as the heavens above shout for joy. Praise Me, trust Me, and hold Me as your own, and the difficulties will pass from you without you being aware of this. Alleluia—you are being set free. Alleluia—trust Me. Alleluia—love Me.

39. MY LOVE MESSAGE

And I pray that you , being rooted and established in love,
may have power, together with all the saints, to grasp how
wide and long and high and deep is the love of Christ
Ephesians 3:17–18, NIV.

The following was received on Valentine's Day!

*T*his is My love message to you. On a day when humans send messages of love to one another, your God sends one to you. Do you have any idea how deep My love is for you? You do not have any idea how long, high, or deep My love is for you. I traveled further than anyone would go for you. I suffered more pain than anyone would suffer for you. I am still wooing you each day, because I can hardly stand not being with you in all you do. Man has learned love from His Creator. You think it's hard to be apart from the one you love; you can't imagine life without your loved one. That is all learned from the heart of God. I can't imagine you not being with Me for all eternity. Remember, you said yes to Me. You betrothed yourself to Me. You are My bride, and I am yours. Nothing will ever separate you from Me. I will love you with an everlasting love—a love so enduring that time and space cannot even fill it—a love that knows no bounds, no stagnation, and no ending. You are My love.

40. MY SPIRIT WILL FIGHT FOR YOU

For the battle
is
the Lord's *1 Samuel 17:47, NKJV.*

*T*rust—perfect trust—can keep one calm. Many want to disrupt My people. The battle is not always flesh and blood, but spiritual. My Spirit is upon you. You must yield to My Spirit to fight for you. Never fear man. The battle has already been won. Trust Me absolutely. The battle is the Lord's. Your job is to trust and remain calm. My Son won over every battle. He sits at My right hand to judge the living and the dead. Only those who have remained in Him shall live. My seal will keep you. You have been given the seal of ownership—My Spirit. He controls you. Yield to Him. He will help you daily, direct you, strengthen you, and uphold you. Oh, if My people only knew all that was available to them in strength and might, they would never fear a thing. "Not by might, nor by power, but by My Spirit, saith the Lord." (Zechariah 4:6 NKJV). Commit the weak into My hands. Commit yourself there, too. Trust—perfect trust—will keep one calm. I love you.

41. WALK SLOWLY

The steps of a good man are ordered by the Lord,
and He delights in his way Psalm 37:23, NKJV.

Walk slowly with Me. There is no rush or fast pace in My kingdom. Everything is orderly, quiet, and peaceful. This can be your life with Me now. Go quietly from task to task, trusting My help and presence in everything you do. Your strength will be in quietness and confidence. I am with you.

V

Freedom

42. DON'T RETALIATE

Seek the Lord while He may be found, call upon
Him while He is near Isaiah 55:6, NKJV.

*B*ring Me your cares, fears, worries, and anxieties. I, alone, can take care of them. I alone can change them and make them what I know they should be. I am your great burden-bearer. Give to Me your every fear, worry, and anxiety. Let Me alone handle it for you. Don't try to get back or retaliate in any way, as that would make matters worse. I, too, am a jealous God. I want My children's undivided attention. I don't want them looking to others for answers. This breaks My heart. Come to Me, all you who are weak and heavy-burdened, and I will give you rest. My children need Me alone to help them. I love you more than you could ever grasp. Come to Me often, and I will help you, uphold you, strengthen you, and love you. Come to Me. I love you.

43. PUT YOUR AFFAIRS INTO MY HANDS

Trust in the Lord, and do good;
dwell in the land, and feed on His faithfulness
Psalm 37:3, NKJV.

Be still and know that I am God. Besides Me, there is no other. The way seems unclear to you, but I am in control of your affairs. You have placed them into My hands; trust Me absolutely. You are being led in a very definite way. My plans will unfold daily as you put your affairs and those you love into My hands. I will keep you connected as you look to Me. Quiet yourself. The busy life is not for everyone. I need you to look to Me. You cannot hear Me when I am crowded out by the noise of the world. Be still and know that I am God. I love you.

44. I AM THE POTTER

But now, O Lord,
You are our Father;
we are the clay, and You our potter;
and all we are the work of Your hand Isaiah 64:8, NKJV.

Your direction in life comes from Me. I am controlling your affairs. You are the clay; I am the potter. I am the architect. I am the master maker of all. Your heart is troubled again about the direction and affairs of your life. You want to know where you belong, what church, etc. You already belong. I made you to belong. Where you fit in is in My dealings with you. I give favor here or there, but real direction comes from My Spirit. You are being buffeted by the world. My hand is in it all. You will see My set purpose on all you do as I lead you to safer ground. Come, follow Me; you must want to please Me in all you do. That is My secret for you. Ask My Spirit for His strength to please Me in all you do. I love you. Go forward unafraid.

45. YOU DON'T NEED APPROVAL

Salvation is found in no one else, for there is no other name under heaven given to men by which we must be saved Acts 4:12, NIV.

*I*n Christ alone, you have your strength. He is your only source of strength, hope, and direction. Look to no other source. It doesn't lie in a job, a ministry, in prayer, or in Bible reading. It lies in Christ alone and what was already accomplished at Calvary on the cross. It's all been done. You can't add a single thing.

You feel drained because you think you must look to yourself for answers. Rest in Me, rely on Me, hope in Me, and love Me. This is all hitting you because you are relying on your own strength to see you through. You try to be everyone's savior. There is only one Savior—Jesus Christ the Lord. You must put aside all and rest in Me. Put all thoughts for the morrow into My hands. Now I want you to put all those you are concerned for into My hands. I will put into your hands what you need to keep you calm and at peace. You try to live up to others' expectations of you when I am the only One to look to for your approval. You don't need approval. You just need My love, counsel, deliverance, help, and direction. You just need Me. I love you. Rest in Me.

46. YOU ARE THE CLAY

***Draw near to God and He will draw
near to you** James 4:8, NKJV.*

You have told Me that you wanted Me to be closer to you—that you also wanted Me to use you as a light to others. As you draw near to Me, My Word will draw near to you. I am the potter; you are the clay. Draw near to Me, and I will mold you and shape you into what I want you to be and what you want to be. Be still and know that I am God. Keep still, and you will know Me as you have never before known Me. Trust and be not afraid of drawing near to Me.

47. RESTORE

*Rest in the LORD, and wait patiently
for Him Psalm 37:7 NKJ*

*W*hen the world seems to crowd about you, when you see yourself becoming overwhelmed with its demands, retreat back to the inner sanctum with Me. I know My children well. I know when you need to rest. That is why you need the inner sanctum of My Spirit to comfort and strengthen you. The pressure of life comes as a result of tiredness, being overworked, not taking rests in between to restore the inner spirit. Let My Spirit restore you so that you can continue on in My strength and love.

48. IN QUIETNESS

Let everything that has breath praise the
Lord. Praise the Lord! Psalm 150:6, NKJV.

*I*n quietness and in confidence is your strength. The plans I
have for you are sure, safe, steadfast, and trustworthy. I will
allow you to see and do great things. Remember always to give Me
all your praise and trust. I alone can do mighty things through you
if you allow Me.

49. WATCH AND SEE

Oh, taste and see
that the Lord is good;
blessed is the man
who trusts in Him Psalm 34:8, NKJV.

My children,

watch and see the

goodness of the Lord.

Remember,

only through Me

can you do

and find

good work.

50. I AM THE WAY

But the righteous are bold as a lion Proverbs 28:1, NKJV.

*J*esus desires you to speak of Him unwaveringly, without fear, and boldly to those He brings before you. They must know Him. How can they know if no one speaks of Him boldly? They think they know Him. They even want to know Him, but they can't unless someone introduces them and shows them the way. I am the way, the truth, and the life. No one comes to Me unless I draw them. Pray I draw all men unto Me. I love you.

51. MY PEOPLE ARE HUNGRY

I am the way, the truth, and the life. No one comes to the father except through Me John 14:6, NKJV.

M y people are hungry to hear the Word—the truth. Speak the Word—the truth—in Love. My Word is truth. It is the only truth to hold on to. My Spirit will guide you into all truth. He is sure, strong, and steady, and He will make you the same. Trust Me. I love you. My Word is truth.

VI

Peace

52. TRUST ME TO ACCOMPLISH

Which of you by worrying can add one cubit to his stature? Matthew 6:27, NKJV

Why do you worry when you know I have you and all your affairs in the palm of My hand? I will see to it that My children will reach their goal. The goal is eternal life with Me. No one will be able to stand against My perfect will for you. Trust Me to accomplish all that I have for you to do. I will perfect that which concerns Me—you. Put the ones you love into My hands. I will see them reach their goals as well. All is well. I love you.

53. YOUR ROOTS ARE GOING DEEPER

That you, being rooted and grounded in love, may be able to comprehend with all the saints what is the width and length and depth and height-to know the love of Christ which passes knowledge Ephesians 3:17–18, NKJV.

*B*e still ... be still. I have many things for you to do, but let Me go on My timing. You just rest in Me; stay very near to Me. I am your stronghold. Nothing and no one can harm you. Your roots are going deeper, but you can't see them or feel them—just like you can't see them in a plant—but they eventually come up, blossom, and produce fruit. So it is with you. You are growing in the night. My Spirit is upon you. Sometimes you feel His anointing; sometimes you don't. He is upon you and seals you. My stamp of ownership is upon you. I shall accomplish what concerns Me.

54. KEEP YOUR HEART FREE FROM SIN

If we confess our sins, He is faithful and just to forgive us our sins and to cleanse us from all unrighteousness 1 John 1:9, NKJV.

My sheep know My voice and obey Me. I am the Alpha and Omega; all things begin and end in Me. Keep your heart clear from the stain of sin so I can use you as My instrument of reconciliation and peace. My sheep know My voice and obey. Listen to Me when I call you and obey. My peace is upon you.

55. RELY ON ME, YOUR DELIVERER

And the Lord will deliver me from every evil work and preserve me for His heavenly kingdom. To Him be glory forever and ever. Amen! 2 Timothy 4:18, NKJV.

You see the enemy surrounding you, attacking you, and provoking you to repay evil with evil. This is what they want you to do, and then they he have you. Rely on Me, your Deliverer, to rescue you from surrounding attacks. My Spirit is very capable to teach and show you the truth. He is the Teacher, Guidance Counselor, and Author of your walk with Me. Trust Him.

56. YIELD TO HIM

You are worthy, O Lord, to receive glory and honor and power; for You created all things, and by Your will they exist and were created Revelation 4:11, NKJV.

*B*e not afraid. I am with you, controlling you by My Spirit. Trust and be not afraid. The Spirit is willing to take control. All you need to do is yield to Him. My Spirit is upon all you do if you are willing to yield to Him. Never doubt My power. It is greater than any force inside and outside of this sphere. My power is made manifest through you as you yield to My Spirit. Call upon Him daily, moment by moment. He will take charge (control) of every situation if you ask Him. He will change the course of events as you pray and ask Him. Trust Me, and be not afraid. I am the Lord of the universe.

57. I WILL MOVE MOUNTAINS

'Not by might
nor by power,
but by My Spirit,' says the Lord of hosts
Zechariah 4:6, NKJV.

You are My chosen one; you are My own. Be faithful to Me and go out for Me. I will go before you to move mountains. I love you. You will see hundreds coming to Me. I alone move hearts and minds towards Me. You are moving in the path I have set before you. Keep moving steadily along, and in due season, you will see every prayer come to pass. Not by your might nor by your power, but by My Spirit, this shall come to pass. I am coming.

58. MOUNTAINS OF DIFFICULTY

The mountains melt like wax at the presence of the Lord, at the presence of the Lord of the whole earth Psalm 97:5, NKJV.

*B*e quiet before Me ... listening, resting. Yes, My children need to be still and quiet before Me so they can know that I alone am God. I make the blind see, the deaf hear, the lame walk, and the hopeless fill with hope and direction. Yes, this is what I want to do through you. Be quiet before Me; be at rest. Have peace, be still, and know I alone am God. Your mountains of difficulties can be pushed out of the way easily through Me alone. You don't need man's help. You only need Me to accomplish all that I have planned for you to do through Me. My Spirit confirms you are Mine. Come to Me often and find rest and peace. I alone am in control of all.

Do you want direction? Then ask Me, and I will have My Spirit show you what to do. Do you want My will? I will show you where to go and what to do. Trust Me in this. Because you ask, I will show you what to do and where to go.

59. I AM THE CONTROLLER

In quietness
and in confidence
shall be your strength   Isaiah 30:15, NKJV.

*B*e quiet before Me; have perfect peace and calm. I want you to quiet yourself before Me. It is then I can minister to you, strengthen you, uphold you, and direct you to what I have planned for you to do for Me. In quietness and in confidence shall be your strength. Be at peace, for I am the Lord of the universe—Lord of all the happenings of your day and your life. I am the controller of all your affairs. Quiet yourself before Me. I love you.

60. I SMOOTH THE ROAD

*No good thing
will He withhold
from those who walk uprightly* Psalm 84:11, NKJV.

*T*rust Me to see you through. No good thing will I withhold to them who walk beside Me, trusting all the way. The way may seem rough, but I smooth the road ahead, softening hearts to help and encourage along the way. Yes, I am in control of your affairs.

61. THINGS THAT HINDER

But endure all things
lest we hinder
the gospel of Christ   *1 Corinthians 9:12, NKJV.*

You are on your way into the deeper life with Me. The Holy Spirit is taking you by the hand and leading gently, step by step, in your walk with Me. He is making those areas that have been hidden more apparent to you now so you can look at them and get rid of those things that hinder and block your way to more of Me. Praise and trust Me. You are on your way. I love you with an everlasting love.

VII

Security

62. YOUR HEAVENLY FATHER KEEPS YOU

Rejoice in the Lord, O you righteous! For praise from the upright is beautiful. Praise the Lord with the harp; make melody to Him with an instrument of ten strings. Sing to Him a new song Psalm 33:1–3.

*I*n everything you do, *trust Me* to show you who loves you. By trusting, you will grow in My Spirit and love. Rejoice in this day, but rejoice more that your heavenly Father keeps you and has kept you always for Himself. Every day is worth rejoicing in that. Come before Me always with singing and rejoicing.

63. CHOICEST OF MORSELS

But it is good for me to draw near to God; I have put my trust in the Lord God, that I may declare all Your works Psalm 73:28, NKJV.

raw near to Me, and I will draw near to you. You are entering upon a new threshold; a new beginning is being formed in your midst. Stand back and watch the Spirit take hold. Don't look to the right or left, but straight ahead. Look in My Word for the choicest morsels of truth. My Word is truth. Cast all your cares upon Me, because I care for you—more than you know.

64. THE WORLD CLAMORS

He will quiet you with His love,
He will rejoice over you with singing
Zephaniah 3:17, NKJV.

Be quiet before Me; be at peace, restful, and still. It is then that I can be heard. The world clamors for your attention, but no attention can compete with Mine. I have the answer to all of life—peace, love, harmony of all. These I can give if you allow Me. Allow yourself time to be still and quiet before Me so I can give you all of these. Be still and know I am God.

65. SUPERSTARS

For a mere moment I have forsaken you, but with great mercies I will gather you Isaiah 54:7, NKJV.

The people of the world look to superstars as their gods—those they want to emulate. I raise up man, and I allow him to be down for a time to look to Me. If man is raised up, very often, he does not look to Me, because he has no need for Me; he has no need for My approval, guidance, and direction. He believes he is controlling his destiny, but My people must always look to Me and trust Me alone for complete direction in every aspect of their lives. How will you know I am controlling your destiny unless you go through periods of almost complete abandonment? It is then that you cry out to Me to show you the way and to have Me more in your life. This pleases Me—to be more in your life. You need Me, but I need you, too—more of you, all of you—for My leading and guidance for the work I have called you to do. Trust Me. Trust that there will always be more of Me as you go on with Me—more of My comfort, more of My love, more of My direction, guidance, leading, and establishing. You are being established by Me. I love you.

66. LACK OF KNOWLEDGE

The Lord is the
strength
of my life Psalm 27:1, NKJV.

M y children are suffering and dying for lack of knowledge of Me. Someone needs to tell them unapologetically and emphatically that they are doing wrong. Their lives can be made right by Me. Tell them to heap upon Me all their sins, cares, worries, and concerns. I am the only one who can make them right; I will if they ask Me. Don't worry always what the other is thinking. Just look to Me to make things right.

67. I AM THE DESIGNER

The Lord is my shepherd;
I shall not want   Psalm 23:1, NKJV.

I am your Father. I take delight in you, as I have made you perfect in every way in My sight. I am the designer of all parts of you—the parts seen and unseen. I am shaping you daily in ways that you cannot see or hear. Each day is a better process than the day before. You are growing in the night. I am watching over you and caring for you in ways you cannot see, but it is happening. Trust Me. I love you.

68. ALL EVIL SHUDDERS

And do not lead us into temptation, but deliver us from the evil one. For Yours is the kingdom and the power and the glory forever. Amen Matthew 6:13, NKJV.

Go your way, and watch for Me in all things. Trust Me to help you. Look for Me, and seek Me early before I get crowded out of the day. I am with you each and every step of the way. Shouts of victory are being heard already at your victory. The evil foe must kneel before the one who walks with Me. I am in you. All evil must shudder at My presence in you.

69. DRAW NEAR

As the Father loved Me,
I also have loved you;
abide in My love   John 15:9, NKJV.

*T*he way seems long and tedious. You are weary because you look to yourself for answers. I am waiting for you to give all to Me. Heap upon Me your weariness and confusion. I am the only one who can make things right. You are entering a stage of victory. All who see will wonder, but you will know who is controlling all for you. Draw near to Me. I need you close to Me. I love you more than anyone or anything could ever love you. This is love you will know more and more. Pray often to receive My love. Receive it and give it. You must receive Me and My love first before you can give out My love. Rest in Me.

70. SHOUTS OF VICTORY

*I will instruct you and teach you
in the way you should go;
I will guide you with My eye* Psalm 32:8, NKJV.

I am the beginning and the end. My Spirit is instructing and pointing the way for you. I have given much to you to prepare you for the work I have for you to do. Already I hear your shouts of victory. I am willing and able to instruct you in the way you should go. Be still and allow Me to speak to you. You are being led in the path I have for you. Trust Me. Just look to Me to supply all your needs. You are not the potter. The potter is very careful with His clay. I do the molding and shaping. I know the exact usefulness for My clay. Every bit is used for My purpose.

71. EXPECT THE NEXT GOOD

Or what man is there among you who, if his son asks for bread, will give him a stone? Matthew 7:9, NKJV.

*M*eet Me in the atmosphere of My love and security. Rest assured that even though the way may be long and toilsome, the way will always be with more and more of Me. I am longing to give you the desires of your heart, but you are always waiting for the next harshness to befall you. I am not a God who expects His children to live in dread of Me and My plans for their lives. I want My children to expect the next best from Me, the next goodness from Me, and the next blessing from Me. I want My children to wrap their arms around My neck as a child does of his or her father, longing for the love, acceptance, and approval I have for you. I want My children loving, trusting, and near Me, as if I am the only one who matters to them. It is then that I can hold you and rock you as a mother does her newborn babe. It is then that I can soothe you and heal you of all your fears and worries. Let Me love you. Let Me heal you. Let Me give you the life I have planned for you from the beginning. Give Me your heart. I will hold it, heal it, mend it, soothe it, and reshape it into My very own heart.

VIII

A Helper

72. TRUST ME COMPLETELY

Because the foolishness of God is wiser than men, and the weakness of God is stronger than men 1 Corinthians 1:25, NKJV.

*D*on't try and figure out My plans for you. I will accomplish what concerns me, as I have told you before. The world will look upon you as foolish, but the *foolishness of God* is greater than the *wisdom of man*. My people long for answers. I give many, but I withhold most so that your faith develops in trust of Me. I long to give you My special gifts to use for Me—yes, like now, to uphold, encourage, and build up My people. That is what it is for. Trust Me completely. I will accomplish what concerns Me.

73. ABUNDANT LIFE

*I have come that they may have life,
and that they may have it more abundantly*
John 10:10, NKJV.

I came to give life—bountiful life. Take it. If you don't receive it, it cannot be given. My children have misunderstood this promise; therefore, many go through life groveling to keep afloat when all they must do is cry out to Me. It is then I take you by the hand and lift you out of your despair and groveling to the abundant life that I have intended for you from the beginning of time. My people don't realize the goodness of the Lord in the land of the living. Cry out to Me, and I will show you what I've intended for you from the beginning of time. You are Mine. I will pour out blessings upon you that you will not even be able to contain. You will have to give much away to be able to contain it all! You are Mine. I provide.

74. WHY DO YOU DOUBT?

O you of little faith,
why did you doubt?   Matthew 14:31, NKJV.

*W*hy do you doubt that I would want to speak to you? I am your Father, Brother, controller of your affairs, lifter of your spirit, guidance director, lover of your soul, matchmaker, harmonizer, peacemaker, and your soul's companion. Wherever I go, you go. Wherever you go, I go. I can transform mediocrity into stardust, bliss, calm, and assurance forever. I am the Transformer. Give to Me all that needs transforming—yourself, your relationships, and your everyday happenings. Let Me show you the way. Walk close beside Me. All is well.

75. JOY-MAKER

For the
joy of the Lord
is your strength   Nehemiah 8:10, NKJV.

Your joy comes totally from Me. I am the Joy-Maker. You have much to be joyful about. I am your Provider. I will always provide for My own, as they look to Me and no other. Try Me in this. I am a God who lavishes beauty and goodness daily for My own. Look around you. See your blessings. Count them. Name them. No good thing will I withhold from those who walk uprightly. I am a jealous God. I will have no other gods before Me. Never look to man; look to Me. I am the most high God. Before Me, there is no other.

76. I WILL LEAD

He helps me do
what honors him
the most Psalm 23:3, TLB.

et Me lead the way for you. Go quietly from one task to the other, trusting Me to help you accomplish each task. Be quiet before Me, and this quiet will bring you much peace. I and the Father are one—one in Spirit. Look to My Precious Spirit for all your needs. He wants to help you trust Him for all your needs. My Spirit has His set purpose for each life. Look to Him to accomplish your set purpose. The world will go from one trauma to another. Choose not to let your heart be troubled or afraid. I and My Father are one. We control the world. Stay close to Me, and I will show you your set purpose and help you accomplish your set purpose. Look to Me. Look continually to Me. Set aside quiet times to rest and replenish in My presence. Go forward unafraid. I am with you, controlling your life. I am your Master and Maker, and I love you.

77. PRAYER AVAILS MUCH

The effective,
fervent prayer
of a righteous man
avails much.   James 5:16, NKJV

I will pour out *My* Spirit upon this need. *Your* prayer and supplication are greatly needed for this soul and the souls of others. *Through* prayer and supplication, with thanksgiving, present this request to *Me*. *How* thankful *I* am that *My* children pray for the needs of others. *Without* these prayers, many would be lost. *You* underestimate the gift and ministry *I* have given you. *Your* prayers avail much. *My* children need the love and support of one another to help each other fight the enemy of their souls. *The* battle is fierce, but the battle is *Mine*. *I* will conquer. *I* will see the souls given to *Me* succeed in this life to attain everlasting life with *Me*. *You* are *Mine*.

78. MY LOVE NEVER FAILS

*Love
never
fails.* 1 Corinthians 13:8, NKJV

First and foremost love the Lord your God with all your heart, mind, soul, and strength. Love yourself. Then love your neighbor. I will give you this love when you draw near to Me. Love never ends; it is eternal. The love I want you to have is absorbed from Me to you when you are near Me. That is why I want you to develop an attitude of quiet and stillness. It is then that My love transfers from My heart to yours. It is then that love transfers from your heart to others all around you. It is then that you are transformed.

79. ONE DAY AT A TIME

*Trust in the Lord, and do good; Dwell in the land,
and feed on His faithfulness. Psalm 37:3, NKJV*

I am here with you. You are learning how to trust Me one
day at a time. In time, this will become a habit and then
automatic. There is no peace or joy like that of trusting Me for the
moment. Every moment. You are drawing closer to Me than ever
before. Calmness, peace, security, love, patience. They all come from
nearness to Me only, one day at a time. Trust Me.

80. TAKE HOLD OF MY WORD AND USE IT!

For the word of God is living and powerful, and sharper than any two-edged sword, piercing even to the division of soul and spirit, and of joints and marrow, and is a discerner of the thoughts and intents of the heart. Hebrews 4:12, NKJV

Seek Me early before the day rushes on. Quiet yourself. Let Me take control. Yes, My word will show you the direction to take. My word has power to demonstrate to the world that its not by might, nor by power, but by My Spirit that causes man to have good success! My word is living and active. It has the power to cut through the mightiest fortress, to pull down strongholds and everything that exalts itself against the knowledge of God. Take hold of My word and use it!

81. DRAW NEAR

But it is
good for me
to draw near
to God; Psalm 73:28, NKJV

raw near, My children, draw near. You wonder why I ask you to draw near. Draw near Me for My love. My love for you, My love for you to love yourself. My love for you to love others. My love will heal you, give you hope, help you, restore you, guide you, direct all your steps. My love will open up doors for you that no man can close. My love is all you need. Draw near, My children, draw near.

IX

Truth

82. SHOW THEM MY COMFORT

Blessed be the God and Father of our Lord Jesus Christ, the Father of mercies and God of all comfort, who comforts us in all our tribulation, that we may be able to comfort those who are in any trouble, with the comfort with which we ourselves are comforted by God. 2 Corinthians 1:3-4, NKJV

Your heart breaks for these ones whose lives are hurting. They need the Savior. They need Me. Yes, pray for them; pray they turn to Me. Cover and support them with your prayers and loving compassion. With the comfort that I have comforted you, show to them. Yes, the God of all comfort wants to comfort them. Thank you for praying for their needs.

83. LET THE WORLD SEE ME THROUGH YOU

*You will
make me
full of joy
in Your presence.* **Acts 2:28, NKJV**

*M*y Spirit is upon you to anoint you to bring good tidings to the poor, bereft, and despondent. I will go before you. Trust Me to prepare your way. I see up ahead. I know men's hearts. I, too, can change men's hearts. I want the world to see Me through you, to see My ways through you. Come to Me often and let Me comfort and assure you of My presence in your life. One step at a time is all you need to walk. Trust Me. I will go before you. Now rest in My presence.

84. MY SPIRIT IS LEADING

As for God,
His way
is perfect; Acts 2:18:30, NKJV

You are going in the direction I have planned. I will support you, lead you, guide you, strengthen, and comfort you. My Spirit is leading. Let Him lead. Give Me your perfect trust.

85. YOUR HEART CRY

My soul
thirsts for God,
for the living God.   Psalm 42:2, NKJV

What makes you think I don't hear you—that I don't hear your heart cry? I am leading and controlling your affairs. Your life is my concern. You gave Me your life. Now look to Me to lead the way.

You want to do much for Me. When the time is right, you will do much for Me. The way seems unclear, foggy, uncertain. Don't fear. I am in control. I will accomplish what concerns Me. Look often to Me...long for Me as a dying, thirsting man in a desert. I will meet your needs. You will hear, well done thou good and faithful servant, enter into My kingdom. All is well.

86. ETERNAL LIFE

These things I have written to you who believe in the name of the Son of God, that you may know that you have eternal life, and that you may continue to believe in the name of the Son of God. 1 John 5:13-14, NKJV

Yes, I always was, is, and forever shall be, eternal. That is how life was meant from the beginning—Eternal. Man was not designed to die, but to live forever. Now he who believes in Me, relies upon, trusts in, will live forever—with Me. My people perish for lack of knowledge of Me. Pray, pray, pray that the veil will be lifted from the eyes of those who don't believe yet. I am coming soon!

Your loving Savior, Jesus

87. TRUTH

*What
is
truth?* John 18:38, NKJV

I am with you to guide you into all truth. My Word is truth. Come with Me into the deeper walk with Me. Abandon yourself into My love and security. Walk with Me, talk with Me, love Me, and let My love fill you to overflowing.

88. PRAY

Pray
   without
      ceasing,   1 Thessalonians 5:17, NKJV

*P*ray, pray, pray for the nations. Pray for the world. My Spirit hovers over you as you pray. He will direct your thoughts. He will direct your prayers. The nations weep as confusion and chaos is rampant. No one knows or seems to care that My children are dying everywhere. Pray for the peace of Jerusalem. Pray for there protection. My Spirit listens to the prayers and intercessions of My children. Prayer warriors are in every nation. My people need to continue to watch and listen to the cries of My suffering people. Your prayers are greatly received. Continue in them.

89. I AM YOUR INTERCESSOR

Therefore He is also able to save to the uttermost those who come to God through Him, since He always lives to make intercession for them. Hebrews 7:25, NKJV

Why are you weeping? Don't you know I am your Father, your Brother, your Helper, and your Intercessor? I am controlling your affairs. I will see you through. I will perfect that which belongs to Me. You belong to Me. I am perfecting you daily. Walk very closely, very gently, for I am planning. I have already planned the present and the future. Walk very near with Me. Give Me your days. Give Me your time. I will plan them for you. Ask Me, and I will help you. I love you. Keep close to Me.

90. REST

Rest in the Lord
and wait patiently
for Him; Psalm 37:7, NKJV

*B*e still, be still and know that I, alone, am God. Do not struggle to find your way. I am the way. If you follow after Me, you will find the way. Life is a struggle if you try and find it on your own. When you put Me first, all else will fall into place. Life isn't all struggle. My world was never intended to put man to the test. Man has found a way to put man first and all else is chaos. My children, rest in Me. Let Me soothe your tired nerves. Rest...stop your feverish running and rest. I will help you accomplish more than you could ever do on your own, if you just put all your cares into My hands. Remember, I can do exceedingly, abundantly, beyond what you could ever ask, think, or imagine. Hold on to Me. I will never let you go. Absorb My love for you. Stay in My presence where there is fullness of joy. Joys unspeakable, and full of glory. All is well.

91. I CHOSE YOU

You did not choose Me,
but I chose you
and appointed you
that you should go
and bear fruit,   John 15:16, NKJV

Near I am to you. Trust Me to see you through. You can't see up ahead. Only I can. Try not to get ahead of My plans. Go one step at a time. I will be there with you on each step, holding, strengthening, and encouraging you. Remember, you did not choose Me. I chose you and appointed you to go and bear fruit; good fruit. Just trust Me on each step you are on.

X

Protection

92. PROMOTION

Let not mercy
and truth
forsake you;

Bind them around
your neck,

Write them on the tablet
of your heart,

And so find favor
and high esteem

In the sight
of God and man.   Proverbs 3:3-4, NKJV

I will promote. *I* will go before you to promote when you look to Me. *I*, alone, can move men's hearts. Better to trust in Me than to put your confidence in man. Trust Me to lead you. Trust Me to guide you. Ask Me for favor with both God and man.

93. THE PERFECTER OF OUR FAITH

Looking unto Jesus, the author and finisher of our faith, who for the joy that was set before Him endured the cross, despising the shame, and has sat down at the right hand of the throne of God. Hebrews 12:2, NKJV

*M*y Spirit is upon you. Rest in Me. Man cannot hear Me above all the noise of his world. Rest and trust can keep one calm. I am the Author and Perfecter of your faith. Remember that. Then you will be able to rest in Me and keep calm. Look to Me. A look suffices. Nothing else is needed.

94. CAST ALL YOUR CARE

Casting all your care
upon Him,
*   for He cares*
*   for you.*   1 Peter 5:7, NKJV

C ast all your cares upon Me. I can bring good out of evil, harmony out of discord, faith out of fear, and hope out of despondencies. Cast all your cares upon Me for I am with you. Trust Me. Don't fear for your life about anything. How can you fear when I am in control? Cast all your cares upon Me.

95. PERSECUTION

*Blessed are you when they revile and persecute
you, and say all kinds of evil against you
falsely for My sake. Matthew 5:11, NKJV*

*Y*our heart is saddened for those you hear that are suffering and dying for their faith and trust in Me. Those who seek me shall find Me, if they seek Me with all their hearts. My children are being cemented to My Spirit. My Spirit will see you through. Yes, My children need to pray for the needs of their brothers and sisters in Christ who are suffering and dying for their faith. But My Spirit will see them through to Me, just as He will see you through to Me. Trust in My Spirit. Love Him.

96. FAITH

Now faith
is the substance
of things hoped for,
the evidence of things
not seen.   Hebrews 11:1, NKJV

Yes, you must have faith in Me. Faith to see you through every weakness, every difficulty, every trial, every unknown. I will be there, always, to see you through. Have no fear. Just perfect trust. You see how I go before you, preparing hearts, giving you favor and confidence in the One who loves you. I am in control. I prepare hearts. I prepare the way for you, so you needn't concern yourself about anything, because I am already there for you. This is called faith—in Me. You are loved.

97. I WAIT

Before I formed you in the womb
I knew you;
  Before you were born I
    sanctified you; Jeremiah 1:5, NKJV

*Y*ou wonder why I wait for you...I waited before time for you to come to Me and share your life with Me. Our life...yours and Mine. Quiet before Me. If only all would take time out to be alone with Me, it is then I could calm their fears, strengthen them, guide their thoughts toward a more desirable way...My way. Speak to Me. I will listen. The time is near when I will reveal Myself in a greater way than before. Lives are still open. Speak out My words. They long to hear them. Recite them out loud. They have power. Power to heal. Power to strengthen. Power to comfort. Power to love.

Come to Me all you who are weary and heavy laden and I will give you rest.

98. THE PERFECT DUO

For we walk by faith, not by sight. 2 Corinthians 5:7, NKJV

J am yours as you are mine. J am in control of all. Abide in Me. Rest in Me. Let Me show you who it is that is controlling your affairs.

Trust and rest are the perfect duo for complete faith. Without these two your faith cannot grow.

99. ACCEPTED

Having predestined us to adoption as sons by Jesus Christ to Himself, according to the good pleasure of His will, to the praise of the glory of His grace, by which He made us accepted in the Beloved. Ephesians 1:5-6, NKJV

Y*ou still look to others for approval. Commit to Me your approval. You cannot be affirmed by men and expect My approval, too. You already have My approval. Man is never going to give you what only I can give. Your approval is based on Me...what I did for you. I gave My life for you. I died on Calvary's cross to give you life eternal, with Me. Look to Me and you won't need man's approval. You have the Holy Spirit's seal of approval when you put your faith and trust in Me and My sacrifice on the cross for your sins. It is then you are approved.*

You will never need more approval than Mine.

100. MY WAYS

For as the heavens are higher than the earth,
so are My ways higher than your ways, and My
thoughts than your thoughts. Isaiah 55:9, NKJV

Looking to Me you grow like Me. Bringing your troubles and concerns and laying them at My feet will lighten your load. I take each one and work it out for the good of all concerned. You remember in the past how I worked things out for you. Trust Me that I will accomplish what concerns you for My glory and honor. Man does not have any idea of the works of God. If he did he would not have a reason to trust in Me...to see him through. I want My children to trust Me for every detail of their lives. It is then you will see My ways.

101. YOU WILL BE HEARD

Yes, and the Lord will always deliver me from all evil and will bring me into his heavenly Kingdom. To God be the glory forever and ever. Amen. 2 Timothy 4:18 LB.

The people who cry out to Me will be heard. I am a God who hears the cries of the human heart. I, too, had a human heart that was heard by My Father. He always heard and delivered Me from all My fears. I and the Father are one. I, too, hear your cries and like My Father, I will deliver you from all your fears. My perfect love will deliver you.

XI

Confidence

102. I AM YOUR DELIVERER

I cry out
with my whole heart;
Hear me, O Lord! Psalm 119:145 LB

The cry of the human heart has many sounds. It could be the sound of anger, or rudeness toward others. This usually is the result of deep feelings of rejection, or being misunderstood. One may not understand why they act or react in this manner, but I know it is the cry of the human heart. The cry of being rejected and misunderstood is a deep hurt.

My people, cry out to Me and I will heal you....I am your Deliverer.

103. HOLD ON

Even there Your hand
shall lead me,
and Your right hand
shall hold me. Psalm 139:10 NKJV

*H*old on in My strength. Hold on to the one who loves you with an everlasting Love. Hold on. Be firm in your stand with Me. I said I would never leave you nor forsake you—yesterday, today, and forever. Hold on to the Prince of Peace. Hold on to the Savior. My Peace is upon you. Quiet yourselves in My Peace.

104. NEADS MET

And it is he who will supply all your needs from his riches in glory, because of what Christ Jesus has done for us. Philippians 4:19 LB

*W*hy do you worry and fret. I continually want to bless your life and the lives you touch. I will supply all your needs. I am the Master-Maker. I know all and fill all your needs. My hand is upon you and all you do. Your loved one, too, is being drawn by My Spirit to attempt and accomplish My work. He will complete all that I have prepared for him to do. I am your Father, faithfully leading you to My kingdom. My children, you are being made ready for My return. Trust on. Go on. I am with you.

105. CLEAVE TO ME

Choose to love the Lord your God and to obey him and to cling to him, for he is your life and the length of your days. Deuteronomy 30:20 LB

*T*he time of all mankind is short. Cleave to Me, your Lifeline. I will see all those who do this, through to the end.

Pray for those who seem to need no help. Pray for those who are forgotten.

Many will come in My name calling Lord, Lord, but only to those who know Me and obey My Word will I answer and have them come into there heavenly Joy awaiting them.

Continue to pray for your world. I am God. I am with you.

106. YOUR PETTY FEARS

I sought the Lord,
and He heard me,
and delivered me
from all my fears.   Psalm 34:4 NKJV

You are My own. You belong to Me. Your petty fears for today and worries about tomorrow are groundless. The Master-Maker is in control of your affairs. You have given them to Him. Your precious, anointed Holy Spirit will guide you, leading you safely through. No problem, no difficulty is too big when He is in control. I remind you, you have already given Him your affairs. They are not retractable. Go forward, My children, to your Promised Land. I am here with you all the way.

107. QUIET LIVES

*This should be your ambition: to live a quiet life,
minding your own business and doing your own work,
just as we told you before.* 1 Thessalonians 4:11 LB

Quiet lives can hear best. Be thankful for your quiet life. You may not hear well on the outside with the noise and clamor of your world, but if you have a semblance of peace, be truly glad. I can only be heard in the quiet places of your heart. Be thankful for your quiet life.

I am getting you ready for My return.

108. GUIDANCE

This also comes from the Lord of hosts, who is wonderful in counsel and excellent in guidance. Isaiah 28:29 NKJV

*M*y children, you lack nothing. You have been given all. When you receive Me, you receive all. Trust Me. Hold on to Me. I am leading and guiding you daily. No one and nothing to harm you. Trust Me and look to Me often. My Spirit is upon you. Receive Him more. He wants complete control and trust. He will lead you. You will know Him more and more. You are being shown the way. Sometimes the way leads to steep steps upwards, but you will be given the strength and joy for the way. Be truly glad for all God is planning for you. A Loving Father delights in His children's happiness. Following Me leads to happiness—real happiness. Joys unspeakable and full of glory!

109. A NEW THING

Behold, I will do
a new thing,   Isaiah 43:19 NKJV

I am your Maker. Try not to figure all out now. I am doing a new thing among the people of God. As they look to Me for their needs, I will supply them. If they look to others to supply their needs, My hand cannot go forth and bless abundantly.

My children need not look to others for their needs met. I am the Author and Finisher of your needs. Don't run, don't fret, don't worry. The world is trying to put it's hold on you. My hand is not shortened that it cannot reach down and save. I, your Lord, your Maker, am going to do a new thing for the people who look to Me to complete their tasks. I will complete every task put safely in My trust. Don't look back. Go forward, unafraid. You will see Me and thus trust Me. I will make sure to you what it is I want done. So don't be afraid. Look up. Look all around. I am here, by your side. You will make the heart of Me glad. You will see.

110. ALPHA AND OMEGA

I have come
that they may have life,
and that they may have it
more abundantly. John 10:10 NKJV

I am the Alpha and Omega, the Beginning and the end. No man comes to the Father except through Me. It is wrong for you to distrust Me. I will answer your prayers if you pray according to My will. I am your beginning to all life and I am the end of all life. Without Me there is no life at all. Ask for the abundant life I have for you. Then you will see fruit...good fruit.

My children need to grow up in Me, to see Me in all their dealings and not to fear man. I am the Author and Finisher of each life given to Me. Stop struggling with yourselves and give Me yourselves. My people perish for lack of knowledge of Me.

You are entering the abundant life. Ask for it. How I want to see the abundance of life fill your every need. I came for this. Receive Me, receive abundance. How I love you.

111. SET APART

In Him you also trusted, after you heard the word of truth, the gospel of your salvation; in whom also, having believed, you were sealed with the Holy Spirit of promise. Ephesians 1:13 NKJV

My Spirit alone makes one holy. Not you. Man cannot make himself holy and righteous before his God. My Spirit sets His seal upon you and He declares you holy and righteous before the living God. It is not what you do, but it is in whom you put your trust. My Son, the Savior of the world, has declared you not guilty before Me. His stamp and seal of ownership is safely seeing you through to your final home. Trust Him and Him alone to give you what you need to make the trip. One step at a time and He will give you what you need to safely see you through. My Spirit is upon you and all you do. Trust Him to see you through. My love is upon you.

112. THE BATTLE IS THE LORD'S

Then all this assembly shall know that the Lord does not save with sword and spear; for the battle is the LORD'S and He will give you into our hands. 1 Samuel 17:47 NKJV

You are My holy ones. To you I have given the secrets of the universe. My people are preparing for battle. My anointed ones are going forth to preach the gospel...a gospel of peace, love and holiness, through My Son, the Holy One of Israel. You, too, are My holy ones. I have made you holy. My Holy One is renewing you day by day. Put your confidence in Him.

My children, come before My presence with singing, and with the Joy of the LORD in your hearts and minds. It is then that I will lift you higher and higher.

Prepare for battle, but know the battle is Mine. I am in control. When you look to Me you will always win! You are being made ready. You are being made whole. The battle is Mine and I have already won!

Jesus is Lord. Come, Lord Jesus!

Here is another opportunity for you to receive a Miracle in your life.

Lord Jesus, I want to know You in a personal way. Please come into my life and make Yourself known to me. I make You the Lord and Savior of my life. I ask You to forgive me from all my sinful ways. I ask that Your Holy Spirit would help me to live a life that honors You! In Jesus Holy Name, I pray, Amen.